Sid and the Scarecrow Dare

orthcott School

Written by Paul Shipton

Illustrated by Jess Mikhail

Sid and Nan went camping.
"I am going to have a nap here," said
Nan. "Go and look at that cow near
the bush, Sid."

Sid went to look at the cow.
It stared back with big, brown eyes.

Then Sid went to make friends with the boy in the next tent. His name was Sam.

"Let's play Dare," said Sam. "I dare you to go and wear that scarecrow's hat! Or are you scared?" Sam jeered.

Sid marched to the scarecrow.
Carefully he reached for the hat.
But then ...

"Beware!" cried the scarecrow.
Sid fell back in surprise.

A girl peered at Sid from behind
the scarecrow.
"It was just me," she said.
"That is my sister," Sam laughed.

Sid was cross. He had torn the
back of his jumper.
"Look at that tear!" jeered Sam.

Sid glared. But then he smiled.
"Be careful, Sam!" he cried. "There is
a bull behind you!"

"You can not trick me," sneered Sam.
But then there was a snort behind him.

Sam turned around.
A pair of big, brown eyes stared at him.
"A bull!" cried Sam.

Sam ran so quickly that he tripped and fell. Now Sam had a tear in the back of his shorts!

"Run!" cried Sid. "The bull is behind you!"
Sam kept running. He was scared.

Nan was awake. "That careless boy has torn his shorts," she said. "Look! Is he running away from a cow?"

Sid smiled cheerfully.
"Oh. Is that a cow?" he said.